THE WESTHILL PROJECT I

MUSLIMS

1

GARTH READ
JOHN RUDGE

Muslim consultants

Rashida Sharif

Ghulam Mustafa Draper

M·G·P

MARY GLASGOW PUBLICATIONS

Published by Mary Glasgow Publications Limited,
Avenue House, 131–133 Holland Park Avenue,
London W11 4UT.

Typeset in Great Britain by Anneset,
Weston-super-Mare
Printed in Great Britain by W S Cowell Ltd,
Ipswich

British Library Cataloguing in Publication Data

Read, Garth
  Muslims.
  1
  1. Islam — For schools
  I. Title II. Rudge, John III. Series
  297

ISBN 1–85234–073–8

Acknowledgements

The authors and publishers are grateful to
the following for permission to use copyright
material:

Photographs

Cover:
Jerry Wooldridge, Garth Read (mosque)

Inside pages:
Jerry Wooldridge pages 6, 7, 8 (left and
middle right), 9, 13, 14, 15, 16, 17, 18, 19, 20,
22, 24, 29, 30, 32, 33, 34, 44, 45, 46, 48, 49, 54
Garth Read page 8 (top right)
Peter Sanders page 8 (bottom right), 35
I.P.A. Picture Library page 60

The illustrations on pages 5, 6, 28, 31, 43 and 59 are by Jane Bottomley, on pages 10, 11,
12, 36, 38, 39, 40, 41 and 42 by Hemesh Alles and on pages 25, 26, 27, 50, 51, 52, 53, 55,
56, 57, 58, 61, 62 and 63 by Peter Wilkes. The maps on pages 21 and 60 are by Ian Foulis.

Contents

1 Belonging

Everyone belongs somewhere.
Where do you feel you belong?

In your family?

In your class?

In your school?

We belong in our city, town or village.
We belong in our country.
We belong in our world.

Miss Jane Packer,
3, Oak Tree Close,
Salford,
Nr. Manchester,
England,
The World,
The Universe

People who belong together are a community, but people
in a community are not all the same. They can be different
in many ways. Can you think of any?

Muslims

Many people belong to Muslim communities.

Muslims are people who belong to the religion of Islam. Muslims are not all the same.

Muslim communities are groups of people who belong to the religion of Islam.

Places where Muslims meet

Muslims like to meet together, and they have special places where they meet.

These places do not all look the same, but they do have the same name. Do you know what it is? You will find it at the top of the next page.

The mosque

Each of the pictures opposite shows a mosque.

Mosques are places where Muslims meet together.

Mosques are places where Muslims enjoy being with their friends.

Mosques are places where Muslims meet for prayer.

Mosques are places where Muslims learn about God.

Mosques are places where Muslims help other people.

Emma and Tracey visit a mosque

Nusrat had invited her friends, Emma and Tracey, to visit her mosque. Neither of them had been to a mosque before.

Nusrat was seven, and she was still learning about the mosque.

She met Emma and Tracey at the front of the mosque and they all went in together.

Nusrat stopped just inside. 'We all take our shoes off before we go in,' she said.

'Why?' asked Emma.

'It helps to keep the mosque very clean,' said Nusrat.

When they were inside, Tracey asked Nusrat why there were no chairs.

'Because we need lots of room to move about when we pray,' explained Nusrat.

Tracey whispered to Emma, 'We have long rows of seats in our church. I don't like sitting on the floor.'

'What are those people doing?' asked Emma.

'Before we say our prayers, we have to wash our mouths, noses, faces, arms, heads and feet,' answered Nusrat.

'Why?' asked Emma.

'Because we want to be very clean when we pray.'

'Boys and girls say their prayers in different rooms,' said Nusrat, and she took her friends to a room where some women were praying.

'This is where I pray with my mother when we come to the mosque.'

'Follow me,' said Nusrat. She took her friends to the front of the mosque.

'We all look in that direction when we say our prayers together,' she said, pointing to a special place in the wall. 'It faces towards the city of Makkah.'

'The man who leads our prayers stands at the front. Sometimes, he stands at the top of those steps to talk to the people.'

'I like your mosque,' said Tracey.

'Come on,' said Nusrat. 'Let's go and play now.'

Have you ever been to a mosque? If so, perhaps you could tell your friends about it.

Muslims do many interesting things when they meet together at the mosque, but the most important thing they do is *pray*.

Prayer

Praying together is very important for Muslims. They pray at five special times each day.

1. Early in the morning, soon after it is light, before sunrise.
2. In the middle of the day.
3. In the afternoon.
4. Just after sunset.
5. During the night, but before midnight.

Because Muslims believe that praying five times a day is very important, they want to pray at the special times, wherever they are.

Sometimes they pray

in their house,
in the street,
where they work,
at the mosque.

Friday prayer

Most Muslims like to pray together with other Muslims in the mosque. Some Muslims do this every day, but all Muslims try to pray in the mosque on Friday.

This is a special day for prayer in the mosque, and lots of Muslims go there for midday prayer.

Learning about God

Lots of people believe in God and they like to teach their children about God.

Some people think that learning about God is very important.

 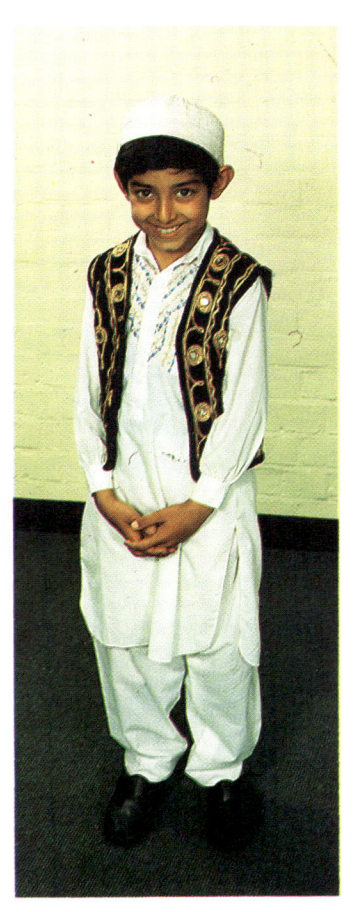

Have you been taught anything about God? If you have, what was it, and who taught it to you?

Muslims believe in God and they teach their children about God. When children go to the mosque they learn about God.

Here are some of the things that Muslim children learn about God.

- God is very great.
- No one is as important as God.
- God is just and kind.
- God does not leave people by themselves.
- God helps people to live as they should.
- God sends messengers to tell people how to live.

God's messengers

Many people believe that God sends messages to people. They believe that God does this in lots of different ways and some believe that very special people have brought messages from God.

Have you heard of Moses? He lived a very long time ago.

Lots of people believe that he was given important messages from God.

Jewish people think that Moses was a very special messenger from God.

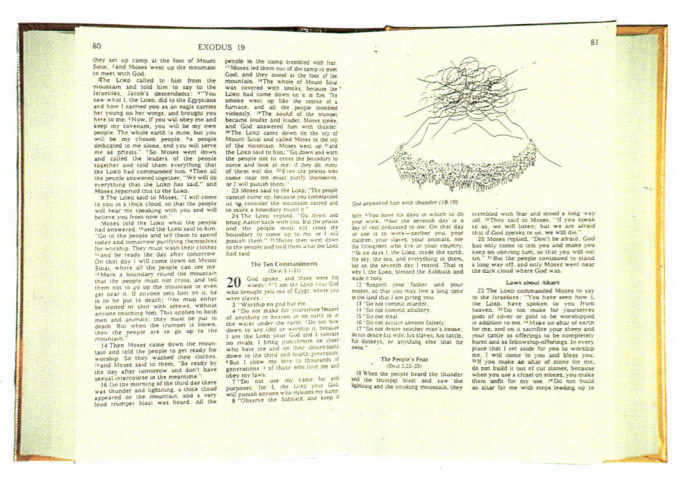

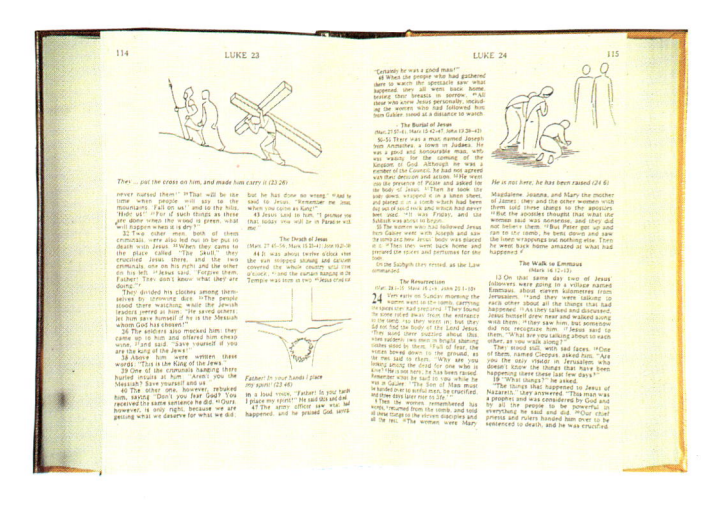

Jesus also lived a long time ago, though not as long ago as Moses. Christians say that he was God's Son and they believe that he brought important messages from God.

Muslims also believe that Moses and Jesus were important messengers of God.

Muhammad

Muslims believe that a man called Muhammad was the most important of God's messengers. Muhammad and the other messengers from God are called prophets.

Most Muslims do not draw pictures of Muhammad because they want people to think more about God than about the man, Muhammad.

The message from God is more important than the man who brought it.

God's message to Muhammad is written in a book. Do you know the name of this book? You will find it at the top of the next page.

Qur'an

The Qur'an is the Muslims' holy book. They believe that it is God's most important message to people in our world.

The Qur'an is written in Arabic. Arabic does not look like English.

The Arabic language came from Arabia. You can see Arabia on the map.

Muhammad lived in Arabia a long time ago and it was there that he received God's message.

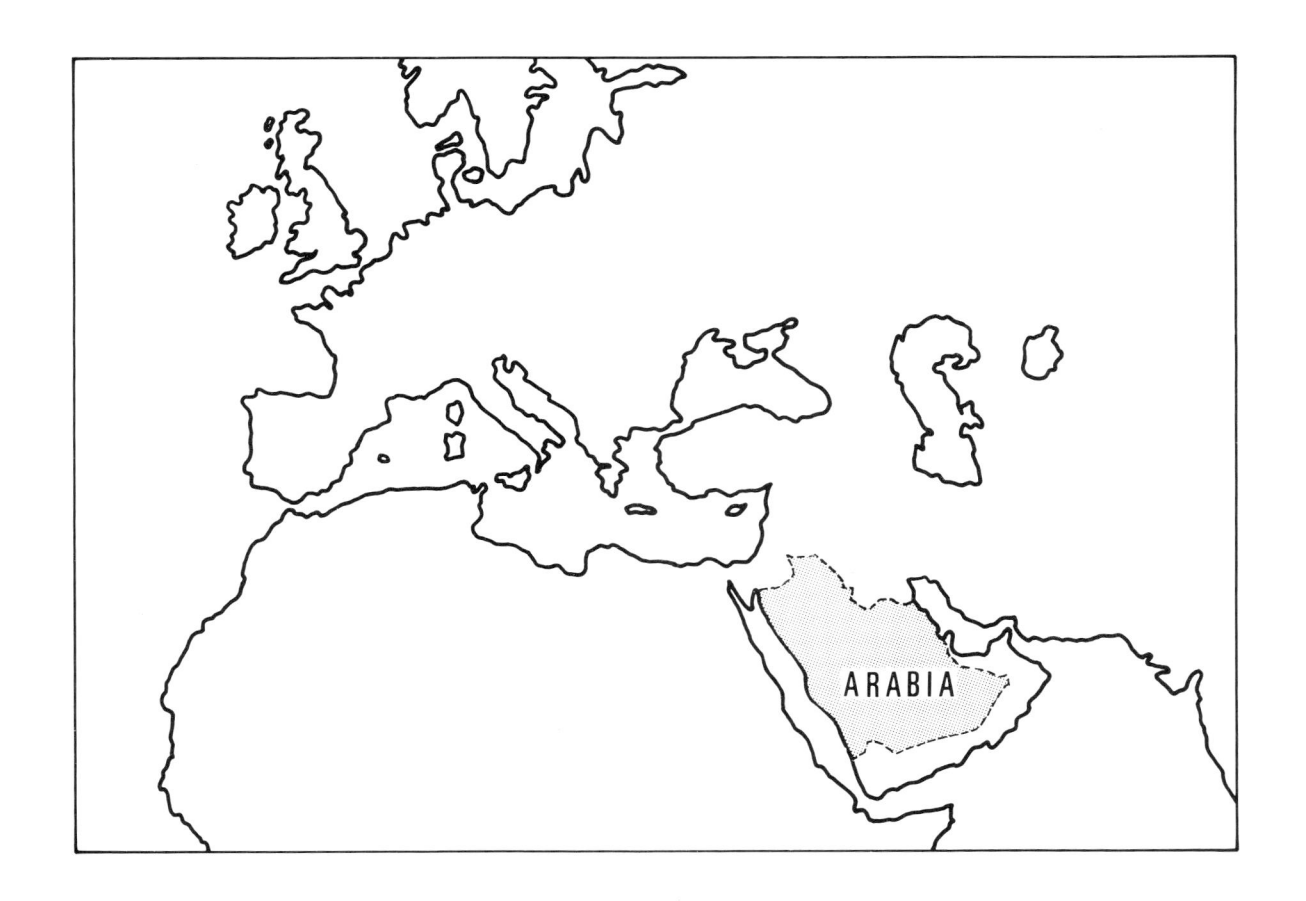

What language do you speak?

Have you ever heard anyone speak another language?
Perhaps you are learning one yourself.

Children who go to the mosque learn the Arabic language.
They learn to read parts of the Qur'an in Arabic.

Here are some words from the Qur'an that Muslim children learn to recite in Arabic.

بِسْمِ اللّهِ الرَّحْمٰنِ الرَّحِيْمِ

These words are called the Bismillah. In English, they mean

In the name of Allah, most Gracious, most Merciful.

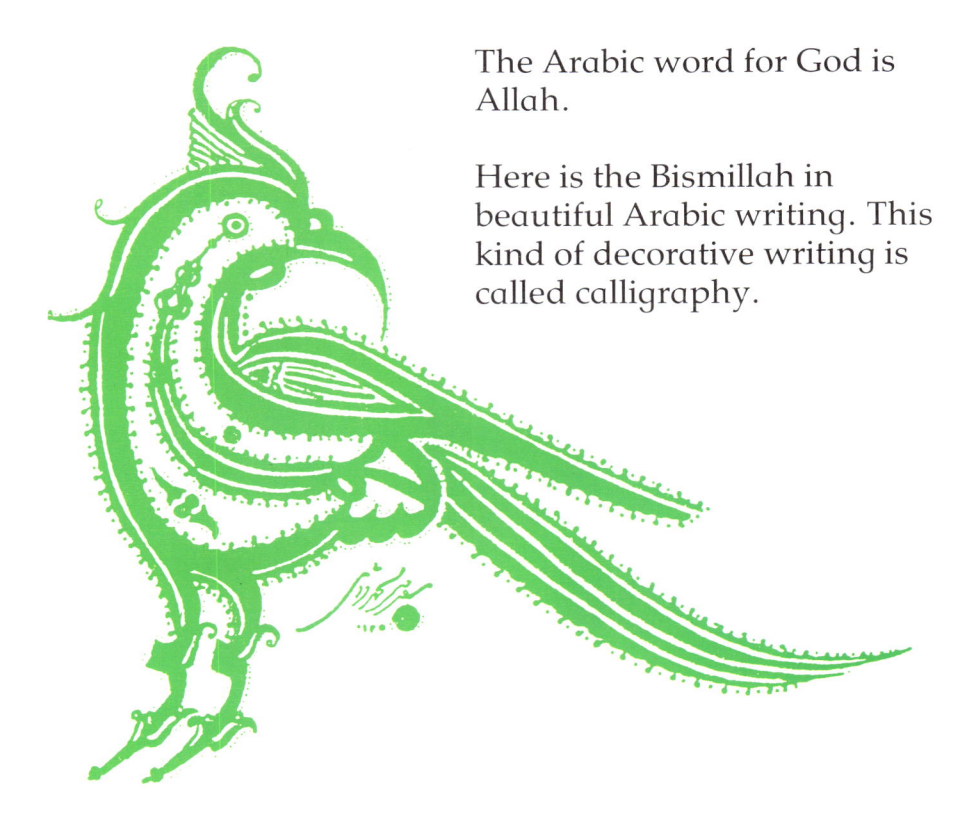

The Arabic word for God is Allah.

Here is the Bismillah in beautiful Arabic writing. This kind of decorative writing is called calligraphy.

Muslim children learn to treat the Qur'an with great care. It is a very special book for them because it contains the words of Allah.

They often wrap the book in a clean cloth. Some Muslims place the Qur'an on a wooden stand when they read it. You can see one on page 20. This helps to keep it clean and special.

Most Muslims learn parts of the Qur'an by heart.

Shanaz and her friends

Jane, Chetna and Shanaz are friends at school. They often walk to school together. One Saturday afternoon Jane knocked on the door of Shanaz's house. When Shanaz opened the door, she said, 'Shh. Shhh. We're going to pray. You can come in and wait.'

Jane went in and sat down. She wondered what Muslim prayers were like.

Soon Shanaz's mother came in. She was drying her hands with a towel. 'Hello, Jane,' she said.

Shanaz and her mother put scarves over their heads. They took off their shoes and put small mats on the floor. Then they stood on the end of the mats.

Just then, Razwan, Shanaz's little brother, ran into the room. He looked shyly at Jane and stood at the end of his mat.

Razwan couldn't keep very still or quiet. He tried to follow Shanaz and his mother as they bowed their heads, knelt down and touched the floor with their heads.

'How do you know what to say and do?' asked Jane, when the prayers were over.

'We try to do what the Prophet Muhammad did,' Shanaz's mother explained. 'We recite some words from the Qur'an.'

'I'll show you our Qur'an,' said Shanaz.

Shanaz's mother watched as Shanaz lifted the Qur'an down from a shelf. It was wrapped in a clean cloth.

'Can I hold it, please?' asked Jane.

'You can only hold it if you wash your hands first. It is a holy book. Let me hold it for you because I've just washed my hands.'

Shanaz held the Qur'an and turned the pages for Jane. Just then, there was another knock on the door. It was Chetna, their friend. Shanaz carefully put the Qur'an away while Jane told Chetna what she had seen.

'I pray with my mother, too,' said Chetna. 'We are Hindus. You can come and see how we pray, if you like.'

'Yes, please,' said the two friends, as they went out to play.

Helping other people

In every community there are people who need help. In every community there are people who help other people.

Have you helped anybody today? Has anybody helped you today?

Muslims helping other people

Lots of people help other people. Lots of Muslims help other people.

Muslims believe that Allah has told them to care for everybody and for everything. They believe that everybody and everything belongs to Allah and that helping people is a way of obeying Allah.

Muslims help people in many ways. One way to help people is to give money.

We can give money to help poor people, or sick people, or hungry people.

Muslims often give money to people who need help. Giving money to help other people is another way of obeying Allah.

Muslims learn that giving money helps people in different ways. It helps the people who are given money to get the care they need. It also helps the people who give it to show their care for others.

It is not easy to be kind and thoughtful all the time. Is there anything that reminds you to be kind and thoughtful?

Sometimes you see pictures on TV of people who need help. Do these pictures make you want to help them?

You have been reading about things that Muslims do together at the mosque. Most of the pictures on this page and the next are about some of these things.

Do you know what the people in each picture are doing? One of the pictures is different because it was not taken in a mosque. Can you spot the odd one out?

a

b

The one on the right in the top line is different. It was not taken in a mosque. It shows a Muslim family at home. In the next part of this book, you can read about some Muslim families.

c

d

e

2 Families

We were all babies once. Your grandfather and grandmother were once babies. Your mother and father were babies once, too. Your brothers, sisters, cousins, aunties, uncles and friends were all little babies once.

Most families are very happy when a new baby is born. They now have a new member in their family and the baby must be given a name. He or she must be given food, kept clean and warm and loved very much.

It is important to make new babies happy and feel welcome.

Muslims welcoming babies

Muslim families have some special ways of welcoming their new babies.

Many Muslim parents want the word 'Allah' to be the first word that their babies hear. As soon as possible after a baby is born, the father, grandfather or a friend whispers into the baby's ears. The very first word he says is 'Allah'. Do you remember that Allah is the Arabic word for God?

Allah is the first word of one of the calls to prayer which are used every day in the mosque. The father whispers these calls to prayer into the baby's ears.

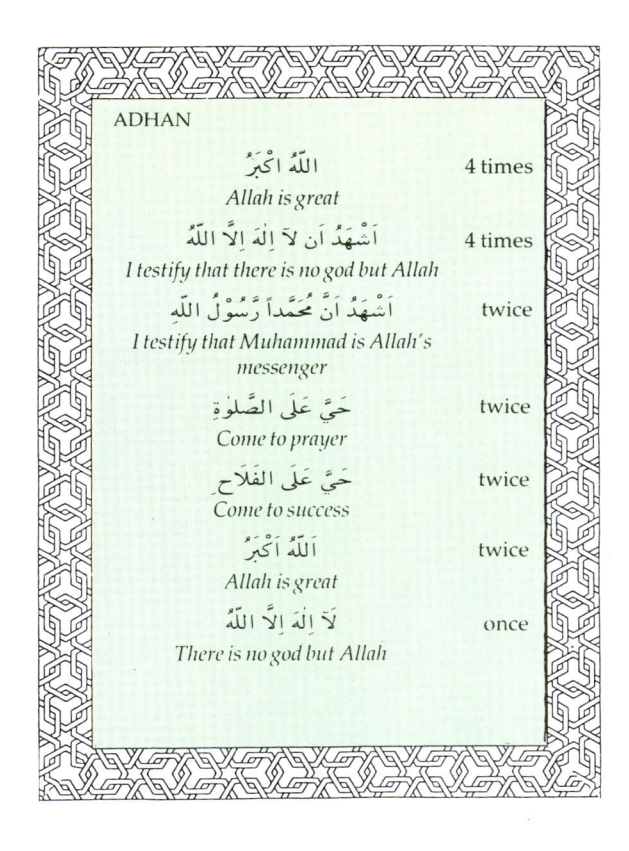

He says this call to prayer into the baby's right ear.

Notice that the word 'Allah' is at the beginning of this call to prayer.

The father says this call to prayer into the baby's left ear.

Notice that the word 'Allah' is at the beginning of this call to prayer too.

You already know the names of the two different languages used in these calls to prayer. One is called Arabic and one is called English. Can you remember why Arabic is important for Muslims?

In some countries Muslim families like to follow an old custom. They put something sweet onto their new baby's lips. They may put a little bit of sugar or honey in the baby's mouth.

They are very careful when they do this because they know that babies cannot eat things that older children eat.

Many parents think that their babies enjoy this sweet taste and they hope that their babies will grow up to enjoy being Muslims as well.

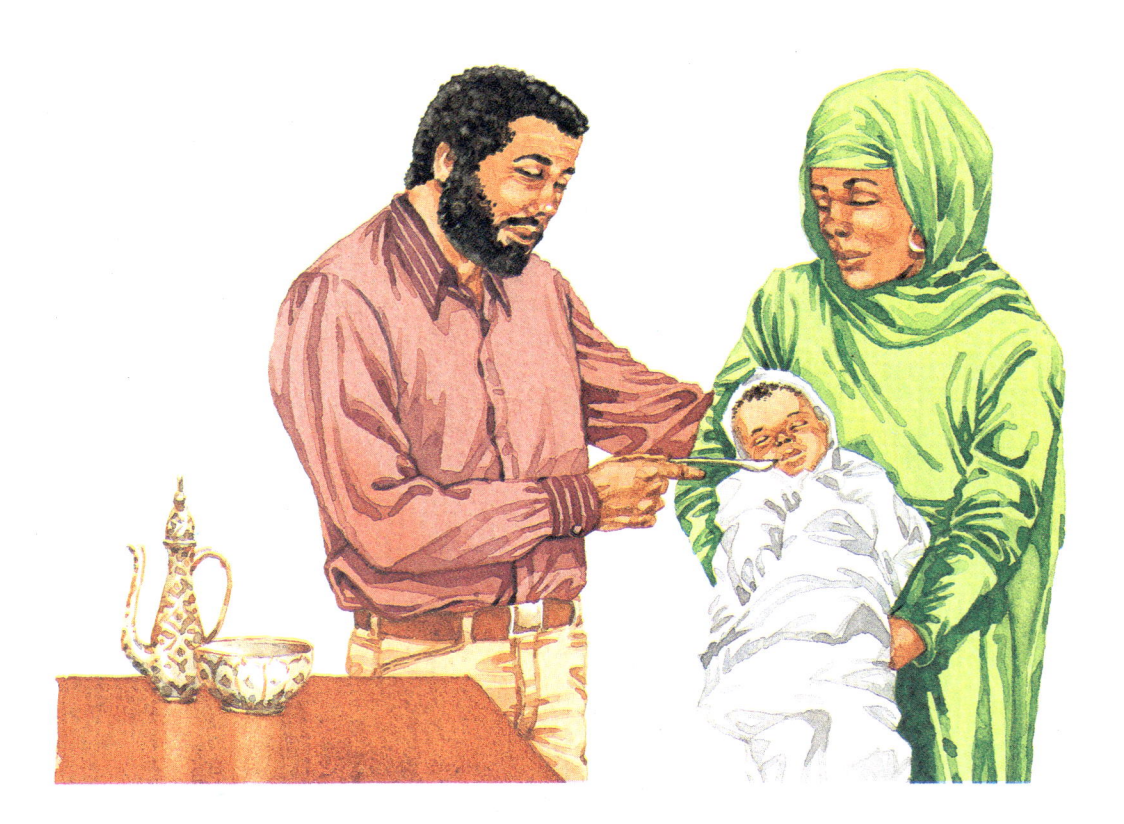

Some Muslim parents get their baby's hair cut off soon
after they are born. They must be very careful when
they do this because they do not want to hurt or
frighten the baby.

Some Muslim parents keep this bundle of hair to remind
them of the day their baby was born.

Abdul Azim is given his name

Asma and her husband, Ziyaad, have had a new baby. Asma's sister, Bushra, is very excited. She is only small, but she is now an auntie.

When the baby was just seven days old, Bushra went with her mother and father and the rest of the family to see Asma and her new baby.

'Do you want to hold him, Bushra?' asked Asma.

'Yes, please!' said Bushra.

She sat down and Asma carefully put the baby in her lap. He felt warm and soft and smelled sweet. The little baby looked up at Bushra with his big eyes.

Soon the baby's father took the little boy into another room. 'The men are going to pray together. Then they will shave the baby's head,' Asma told Bushra.

Bushra heard the baby crying. 'Don't worry, Bushra. Everything is fine. They are just wetting the baby's head before they cut off his hair. They will be very careful.'

Bushra smiled when she saw the little bundle of black hair. Asma weighed it on some small scales. 'I'll give the same weight of gold or silver to help poor people,' said Asma.

'What will you do with the hair?' asked Bushra.

'I'll keep it for a while.'

'In Pakistan our family throws the baby's hair into a river,' explained Bushra's mother. 'That's why Asma has such long flowing waves in her hair.' Everybody laughed and the baby stopped crying.

'Have you thought of a name for the baby?' asked Ziyaad.

'Yes,' said Asma and Bushra's father. 'We asked Grandfather what he thought. He said Abdul Azim.'

'We like that,' said Ziyaad and Asma. 'What does it mean in English?'

'It means "Servant of the Mighty",' replied Bushra's father. 'We chose that name because we hope that he will grow up to be a servant of Allah.'

Bushra smiled. 'I think it is a lovely name for my new baby nephew.'

Celebrating special days

Many families celebrate some important days each year. 'Celebrate' means to make the day special.

They may use colourful decorations, very nice food, games and music in their celebrations and often they like to share these times with their friends.

Perhaps your birthday is an important celebration for your family and friends. Do you have any other celebrations in your family?

Some families celebrate special days which are important for the whole community. Can you think of any?

Muslim family celebrations

Muslims have many important days and many families celebrate these days each year.

You may know the names of some Muslim celebrations. Let's learn about one of them.

Eid ul Fitr

Muslims have a special calendar. There are twelve months in the Muslim year and one of them is called Ramadan.

At the end of the month of Ramadan, Muslims enjoy a time of celebration.

This celebration is called Eid ul Fitr. Eid ul Fitr is a very happy time. It is a time for festival and rejoicing.

Lots of people go to the mosque on the day of Eid ul Fitr. They go there to say special prayers. As they meet their friends, they may say, 'Eid mubarak' or 'Happy Eid'.

Many people give money to the mosque at the time of Eid ul Fitr. Some of this money is used to help hungry and needy people.

Do you remember why Muslims give money to help poor and needy people?

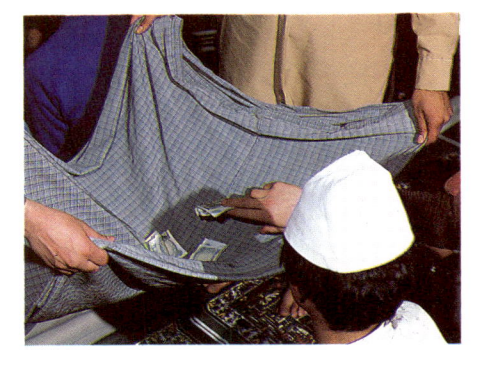

Many people give greeting cards to their friends during Eid ul Fitr. Some may give gifts of money or sweets to their family and friends.

At Eid ul Fitr, Muslims are celebrating something very important. Do you know what it is?

They are celebrating the happy ending of the special month which they call Ramadan. It is a month of fasting.

Ramadan

Do you know what fasting is? It is when people choose to go without food for a time.

Muslims do this each year during the month of Ramadan. They do not eat or drink during the day. They only eat and drink at night.

Fasting during the day for this one month doesn't make them sick, but it does make them feel hungry.

Could you go all day without any food? It isn't easy!

Little Muslim children do not fast, nor do old and sick people. Boys and girls over twelve years old and grown-ups try to fast during the day in the month of Ramadan.

Muslims have a special name for the meal they eat after the sun sets on each day of Ramadan. It is called iftar.

Many Muslims start their iftar by eating a date and having a drink of water.

After eating the date and drinking the water, many Muslim families pray to Allah. Then they may all enjoy the evening meal together. Some Muslims like to go to the mosque to share iftar with their friends.

When Muslims fast during Ramadan and share iftar together, it helps them to know that they belong to the community of Islam.

The fast of Ramadan

Shanaz and Razwan knew that something was different.

Of course, their morning prayer was the same. Each morning when they came downstairs their mother asked them to join in the prayers. They got ready by washing their hands, their mouths, faces, arms, heads and feet. Then they put their mats on the floor. They took off their shoes, covered their heads and joined in the prayer.

But when they went to breakfast, things were very different. 'Why aren't you eating anything today?' Razwan asked his mother.

'It's Ramadan now. While it's light, I won't be eating or drinking anything. I am going to fast each day for a month.'

Shanaz remembered what Ramadan was like last year. 'Soon I'll be older and can fast too,' she thought.

As Razwan went off to school, he thought, 'I wouldn't like to go without food or drink all day!'

Later in the day when they got home from school, it was still light. 'I'm hungry!' said Razwan.

'We'll have a meal later, when Daddy comes in. Can you wait till then?' asked Razwan's mother.

'I think so,' said Razwan, but he wasn't sure.

It was dark when their father came home. All the family ate some dates and drank some water. They prayed and then they had their meal together.

In the morning, when it was still very dark, Razwan woke up because he heard a noise. 'What's that?' he wondered. He knew the noise was coming from the kitchen and he could see a little light under his door.

He got out of bed and as he was going downstairs he heard his mother and father talking. He could smell food cooking. 'What are you doing?' he asked. 'It's still very dark. Are we going away?'

'No,' said his mother with a smile. 'It's Ramadan.'

'Why are you cooking now?'

'Your father and I can't eat when it is daytime during Ramadan, but we have to eat something, so that we can work. So we eat before it is light,' answered his mother.

'Can I have some?' asked Razwan. The smell made him hungry.

'Yes, you can this time,' said his father. 'Then you must go back to bed. You can have your breakfast with Shanaz before you go to school. When you are older and go to the big school, you can fast with us.'

Do you remember why Eid ul Fitr is such a happy time for Muslims?

It is because they are celebrating the end of Ramadan. It means that the fast is over. Eid ul Fitr means, in English, the 'festival of the end of the fast'. Ramadan and the festival which follows are a special time for Muslims, because they help them:

to think about Allah,
to thank Allah for the Qur'an,
to know what it is like to be hungry,
to remember to help needy people,
to try not to be greedy, selfish or lazy.

The fast is over

It seemed a long time since Ramadan began. Shanaz and Razwan were watching the night sky for several days. They wanted to be the first to see the new moon in the sky. They knew that this new moon marks the end of the fast and the beginning of the celebration.

At last they saw the new moon. The festival of Eid ul Fitr could begin.

'Shanaz! Shanaz! Come and help me make the chapattis,' called Shanaz's mother.

Shanaz and her mother are very good at making chapattis. They can throw them from one hand to the other to make them flat and round before they cook them.

Razwan is very good at eating chapattis.

Shanaz was anxious to dress in her new clothes. Her father had bought her a beautiful red set of shalwar and khameez. 'You do look nice, Shanaz,' said her mother.

Razwan looked very smart. He had some new clothes, too. He had a new shalwar and kurthar and he wore these with his velvet waistcoat and white topi.

Then Shanaz and Razwan, with their father and mother, set off for the mosque to pray and to meet friends and relations.

Later in the day, their father took them to a nearby sweet shop. 'I'll have jellebi and some barfi, please,' said Razwan.

'Can we have some now?' asked Shanaz.

'All right,' said her father, 'but they are to share with your friends at our Eid party.'

On the way home they called on some friends.

'Eid mubarak,' they said to each other. They gave their friends an Eid greeting card and told them about the party.

'Come on,' said Razwan, 'we don't want to be late.'

It wasn't too long before the guests started to arrive. 'Eid mubarak! Eid mubarak!' could be heard each time someone came in. When Shanaz's friend, Jane, arrived, she too practised saying, 'Eid mubarak'.

'Come in, Jane,' said Shanaz's mother.

'Come and wash your hands and sit near me,' said Shanaz.

'Do you like our food?' asked Razwan.

'Most of it,' said Jane.

Eid was a very noisy and lively time. As Jane was leaving she thanked them all for inviting her. 'Shanaz!' she said, 'You must come to one of our Christmas parties one day.'

'Thanks,' said Shanaz. 'Goodbye, Jane!'

'Goodbye,' she called back, 'Eid mubarak!'

Journeys

It's exciting going on a long journey. Some people go on a long journey for their holidays. Some people go on long journeys to places of special interest or which are important to them.

Many religious people go on journeys to places where they believe they can be close to God. They often call these places, holy places. Going on a journey to these holy places to feel closer to God, is called a pilgrimage.

Muslims go on a pilgrimage

Do you know where Makkah is? It is a city in Arabia and for Muslims it is a place of pilgrimage. Makkah has many splendid mosques and other buildings. It is a very busy place, especially at the time of the pilgrimage.

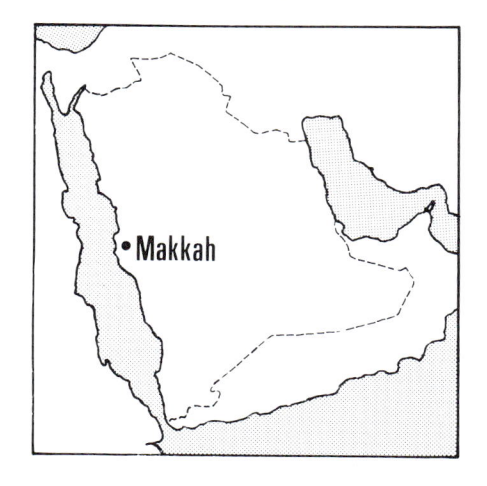

In the court of the great mosque there is a famous building called the Ka'ba. Muslims sometimes call this building 'The House of Allah'. It was built many, many years ago, before the Prophet Muhammad's time. He visited the Ka'ba and now, when Muslims go on pilgrimage to Makkah, they visit it too. It is a very holy place for them.

Mr Rashid packs his bags

One evening when Razwan was getting ready for bed, Mr Ahmed called to see his father. They went into the front room and talked alone. Razwan could hear their voices, and he wanted to know what they were saying. He tiptoed downstairs and listened at the door.

His father and Mr Ahmed were talking about going on a long journey. It sounded exciting. Razwan hoped that he could go too. They were talking about a place called Makkah. Just then, a door opened and Razwan had to scamper back upstairs to bed.

The next day, at tea time, Mr Rashid told Razwan and Shanaz that he was going on a journey to Makkah with Mr Ahmed. 'I'm going to be away for two weeks,' he said.

Shanaz thought, 'I'll be able to stay up later while Daddy's away!'

Razwan asked, 'Can I come too?'

'I'm afraid not,' said his father. 'This is a very special journey. It's only for grown-ups. When you are older, you will be able to make this journey. All Muslims must try to go on this journey once in their lifetime!' Razwan was very disappointed. He had been lying awake in bed thinking about it.

Two weeks later, Razwan woke up early. It was dark, but he could hear his father moving about in the next room. He got up and went in, rubbing his eyes in the bright light. 'Daddy is packing ready to go on his pilgrimage,' said his mother. 'Would you like to help?'

'Yes, please,' said Razwan.

They were putting things into a case. 'What's that?' Razwan asked, pointing to some long white clothes he hadn't seen before.

'It's called an ihram,' said his mother. 'Daddy will wear it when he arrives in Arabia. All the pilgrims will wear an ihram.'

After prayers, they had breakfast, and then Mr Ahmed arrived. Razwan was sad. He would miss his father. He still wanted to go. 'Will you bring me something back?' he asked.

His father gave him a big hug. 'I hope you will think about me while I'm away,' he said. 'This is a very special journey for me. I will tell you all about it when I get back.'

Notes for teachers

This book is the first in the Westhill Project's series of four books about Muslims. It is designed for children of seven to nine years old. Islamic practices and beliefs are described clearly and without bias in all the Muslims books. However, this is done without any assumptions being made about any teacher's or pupil's acceptance of the Islamic faith now or in the future.

Depending on their abilities, some children will be able to read parts of the book for themselves, while others may need more help, or may benefit from having parts read to them. The stories can be read to groups of all abilities, and the pictures accompanying the text may help younger pupils to follow it. In any case, the method you choose will need to suit both the particular children you are teaching and the scheme of work into which you are introducing the book.

There are two parts to the book. Part One introduces children to some of the important features of Islamic communities. In Part Two they learn about aspects of Muslim family life. The Islamic community is dealt with first so that children have some idea of basic Muslim beliefs and practices before they consider the specifically religious aspects of Muslim family life. The two parts are indicated by colour coding around the page number: pink for Part One and blue for Part Two.

In **Muslims 1**, pupils are introduced to several key words and concepts which are considered essential for their continuing religious education:

Human experience words: communities, belonging, needing, sharing, caring, helping, celebrating
General religious words: God, prayer, pilgrimage, belief
Islamic words: Muslims, Islam, mosque, Makkah, Ka'ba, Allah, Muhammad, Bismillah, Qur'an, iftar, ihram, Ramadan, Eid ul Fitr

Content overview of the pupils' books
The four Muslims pupils' books are designed to help pupils develop an understanding of Islam as a world religion. Each book deals with different aspects of Muslim practices, beliefs and experiences.

The diagrammatic presentation below indicates the content of each book and shows how children are helped to build up their knowledge and understanding of this religion in a progressive way from seven to sixteen. The shaded areas in the circles indicate the aspects of Islam dealt with in particular books.

A more detailed explanation of this is given in the teacher's books, **How do I teach R.E.?** and **Islam.**

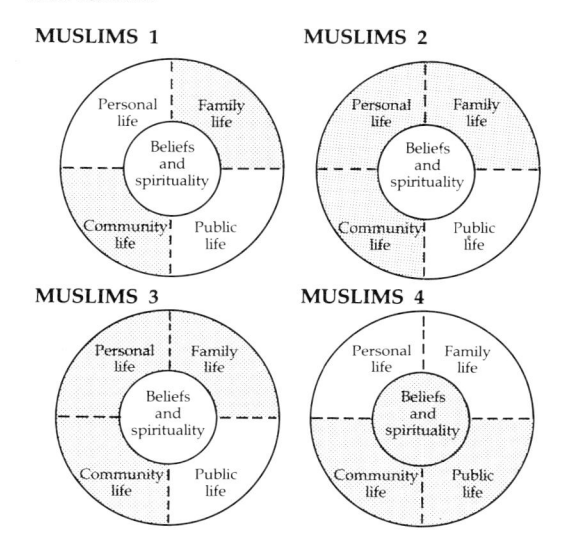

Other materials in this Project
Teachers using this book with junior children should realise that it is only one resource item designed to meet one specific aspect of the primary child's experience of R.E. – learning about Muslims, through the words and concepts outlined above. To expand the range of classroom activities designed to meet this need, a **photo**pack, with additional pictures and information, is also available.

Teachers using these resources are strongly recommended to refer to the two teacher's books: **How do I teach R.E.?** – the main Project manual and **Islam** – a source book and guide to the teaching of this religion. A sug gested scheme of work is to be found in the latter.

Books and photopacks relating to other religious traditions and various Life Themes are also part of **The Westhill Project: R.E. 5–16.**